To Don & Ann
who have their
own Love Poem.

J.C. & Betty
3/5/10

Love Poems

Betty Burton Choate

J. C. Choate Publications
Route 2, Box 156
Winona, MS 38967

ISBN 0-9616352-0-7

Typesetting by Eloise Breazeale Nowell

Dedication

To Ronald and Nancy Reagan,
our beloved President
and his First Lady,
in respect and admiration
for the Love Poem
of their life together.

Author's Foreword

In a sense, Love Poems is the idealized love story repeated over and over again, throughout the world and throughout time. Too often, perhaps, we don't search for the "right" words to adequately express the love of one heart to another. And we get so busy that sometimes the little gestures of love that would help to compensate for the lack of words also fail to materialize. We don't take the time to cherish one another; yet the love, deep down, is there. This search for words to express my own love and the love I see in others has felt sweet in my heart, and the outpouring has brought a sense of completion. I hope that others will find it useful. Love is too monumental a thing for any of us to hold it as a mute prisoner inside our hearts.

Love Poems.....for those who are experiencing the sweetness of young love, for those who have cherished through the years the security of loving and of being loved, for those who have grown old with the wonder of that treasure still new in their hearts.....

September 23, 1985

Table Of Contents

The Gift

How many precious gifts
God gave in love to man:
    Eyes to see
    And vision for the deeper sight,
    Ears to hear
    And, yes, the unseen ear
    To hear the spirit's sigh,
    The voice to speak
    And cries that make no sound,
    The touch of hands
    And touchings of the soul.

God gave them all:
    The outer gifts of man,
    The inner, deeper gifts;
And then, at last,
Along with breath and life
He formed man's inner heart
    And gave the gift of loving.....

The Birth of Love

Looking back
I wonder how it could have been
That normal skies stretched overhead
And common sounds
Of birds and voices
Filled the air
And earthy things
Obeyed the unseen law
As any other day.....
    There was no sound of siren
    ——Not even eerie stillness——
    No warning bell of any kind
    To say the moment neared
    When
    Out of ordinary life
    I raised my eyes
    And saw you standing there;
        One frozen instant
        Lifted out of time
        And made a crystal
        Of eternity,
        That moment
        When the empty vacuum of my life
        Was filled
        And love for you was born.

Alone

Oh, World,
   ...Go away...
   Don't come to talk
   Or sell..
   Don't come intruding in my thoughts...
   Bring me no ring of door
   Or telephone...
   No music——
   Not any sound at all.

   Let me have time
   To close my eyes,
   To close my ears,
   To stop all outer sense of feel
   And concentrate instead
   On all these feelings in my heart:
      This sweetness
      And this dreaming,
      This aching pain
      That must be ecstasy——
         Oh, let me sit here all alone
         And hug this wonder to my soul:
         I love!   I love!   I love!

Precious Thoughts

Not always can I talk of you
For others tire of love
And would not hear
Your virtues always praised.....
    Perhaps they're right,
    Perhaps such things as weather
    Or some distant war
    Deserve some thought as well;
But, oh my love, I hear
With inattentive ears
And turn instead to inward thoughts,
Precious thoughts,
Of all you are
And all you're meant to be
And, deep within, where others never walk
I share a world with you.

Nothing

It's time for you
    To call
    or write
    or come.
I wait.
My pulses quicken,
Waiting,
Believing.
And I wait.

Nothing.

Nothing.

Nothing.

And I die inside again.

Love's First Embrace

You said no words,
And neither, Love, did I.....
You read it in my eyes
And so
With feet that touched no earth
We crossed the space as in a dream
And time stood still
In love's embrace.

I felt the softness
Of your cheek on mine,
My open palms
Against your back;
You held me tightly in your arms
And it seemed
That melting into me
Was all your body's warmth
And strength.

I raised my head
And looked into your eyes
——great gulfs of love——
And lightly
    Like a fragile gift
    Your fingers touched my cheek
    And the whisper of a kiss
    Caressed my lips.

How long we held each other so
I cannot guess,
But the imprint
Of that feeling,
 warm and sweet,
Of your body
Pressed against my racing heart
Has formed a block of time
——a memory, eternal——
Of that first embrace.

Two Halves Of A Whole

We shared an experience
——you and I——
Each of us contributing
Smiles and words,
Expressions, gestures, thoughts,
Reacting and interacting
With each other——
Two halves of a whole experience.

Distance and time have wedged a gulf
——impassibly wide——
Between us, and between now
And the yesterday of our experience.

But I close my eyes
And I see again your movements,
Your smile, your soul in your eyes;
Your words and your laughter
Ring in my ears anew,
And I carry
——here——
A living thing in my heart:
The half that was you
of all that we shared.

Does the half that was me
live.....?

'I Love You'

"I love you."
    You've said the words
    Not as a well-planned speech
    But all alone,
    A simple statement
    Of your heart,
    And I accept it so.

I understand.....
    We've shared so much,
    So many thoughts and dreams
    And tears,
    So much of growing
    In the passing years,
    So many gifts of self,
    So much of hope,
    And now you've crowned them
    With the gift of purest gold:
    ——"I love you"——
    I need no more.

What Does It Mean?

What does it mean,
    This being loved,
    This living in another's heart?
    It's all so new to me.....

Does it mean
    That at last I'll feel secure,
    I'll have no more of doubts,
    No anxious tears,
    No empty waiting in my heart?

Does it mean
    My world's skies will be blue
    In spite of storms around,
    That birds will sing
    And we will laugh in happiness?

Does it mean
    No outside force will ever threaten you,
    Your place within my heart,
    Or mine in yours?

Does it mean
    That always in your arms
    My soul will be at rest?

Is this what loving means?

At Last!

On paths beginning
   in the mists of long ago,
We've come at last upon this day.

   I feel in you
   The things you feel in me,
      the hesitancy, the measuring, the questioning,
   Swallowed up
   As though they'd never been,
   And our spirits see
      exultantly
   That nothing now remains
     of hidden walls
     or bolted doors:
        At last we're free!

   Was it both of us
   Who ran to close the space,
     to stand tight-clasped,
     crying over hurts
     and sorrows of the past
     and laughing
     in the triumph of today,
     the sweetness of our binding kiss
     commingled with the salt of tears?

     At last our love is one!

Without Reserve

Can one truly love
With walls around the heart?
    I think it cannot be.....
   And so I come to you
      Without reserve,
      Without defense,
      Exposed in openness
      And in the tenderness of love,
      Trusting in your love
      To hold with gentle hands
      The heart I give in faith to you.

Photographs And Dreams

Oh, my love,
In a moment caught in time
Arm in arm
We laugh into each other's eyes
And ignore the world around.

Ah——I'd make that picture live
And your other arm, half-raised,
Would pull me close;
Your smile would fade
With slowly lowered head
And a sweet, sweet kiss
Would stir my soul.

Oh, my love, I'd make that picture live.

Oneness

What is this cord
——unseen——
Between us
That reaches out and makes us one?
    How is it
    That I feel your feelings
    In myself,
        Your fears,
        Your hurts,
        Your triumphs,
        As my own?
    How is it that I feel your thoughts,
    The longing in your heart?
    How is it that I look into your eyes
    And see my soul?

Expressions Of Love

Please don't doubt my love
For doubts would melt my heart and make me cry;
Our love is not built on feeble thoughts,
On weakness and on tears,
But on faith,
Unshakable and strong,
Created by God,
Protected by Him,
Living through His love,
As His hands
——unseen by men——
Reach down to us and shape our future years;
Our love is not a line
Drawn in futility on water or on sand:
It is a strong cord
Stretched between two souls;
For you are innocent and truthful,
A darling child of God
And I think
That not before in human history
Has there been a love like ours;
You
And your love
Are the most precious thing
For me,
The most valuable gift of God...
    I love you.

Joy

I want to sit,
   Withdrawn from all around,
   And think of you,
But I feel the world and people
Crowding in
And, so, begrudgingly, I turn to duty,
Giving thought to other things
And, sadly,
Feeling drawn away from you.....

But realization, rich and sweet,
Comes flooding through my mind:
   No outside thing can threaten you,
   You live within my heart
   Caught up in me,
   A part of me,
   A part of all I do and feel,
   As real as those around are real.
   I hear your words, your laughter in my ear,
   I see you move against the background of reality
   And, deep within our private world,
   I feel the joy of knowing
   That no measured time or measured space
   Define the love we share;
   Whatever I may do,
   Wherever I may be,
   I find you there.

That I Can Pray

I search among my treasures.....
   I must find the choicest gift of all
   To bring to you today;
   What can it be?
      Not something that will break
      Or crumble with the years,
      Not words
      Or even something that my hands
      Have made for you alone.....
   What can it be?
      Ah, yes.....
      With purest heart
      And purest love
      I'll go before our God,
      Before His great and awesome throne,
      And bowing there to worship
      At His feet
      I'll breathe your name
      And ask His care,
        His special care,
      For you throughout this day.....

      Sweet, sweet gift of love,
      That I can pray for you!

'Yes' To What?

Today we heard the question
   "Do you take this one...?
   And we answered, "Yes..."

"Yes" to what?
   To waiting ended,
   "Yes" to feeling more acutely,
   To dreaming
   And to sharing dreams,
   To picking up together
   All the pieces
   When the dreams come crashing down,
   "Yes" to happiness enlarged
   And grief diminished
   Through their sharing;
   "Yes" to working for each other,
   Routine work
   And sometimes boring
   But part of life
   And surely part of loving;
   "Yes" to smiles with deeper meaning
   And to hurts
   When quarrels come;
   "Yes" to secret jokes
   And fears we'll share unspoken,
   "Yes" to oneness in our thoughts
   Our goals and our possessions,

In our bodies
And the fruit our bodies bear:
A growing, changing blending
    of us both.
"Yes" to cherishing,
    Obeying,
    For better or for worse,
    Through good times
    And the bad;
"Yes" to growing old together.

In Answer

Across the room
I catch your eye
And the sweetness of a smile
Begins to form
In answer to your own;
But then without a word
The smile is swallowed in intentness
And a current
Like a flashing message from your eyes
Burning into mine
Sparks a kindred fire.

Shared Tears

I came to you,
Hurting,
Needing strength
And words that said
You cared about my grief;
You held me, though,
In silence
While the hurting
Overflowed my soul
And filled my eyes
With salty tears.....

    But, oh, the words you never said
    I heard within my heart
    As gentle fingers cupped my chin
    And made me look into your eyes
    And there I saw my tears.

If I Could...

If I could
I'd shield you, Love,
From every hurt,
The danger in the way;
I'd rather feel your pain myself
And make your life
One long enchanted road of joy,
One thrilling song without an end——
    In the weakness of my love,
    I'd do this, if I could.

But God decrees that growth must come
Through pain as well as joy
And easy roads
Would make you weak and spoiled;
And, so,
Because He loves you
More, dear one, than I
He marks the way that's best
For you
And helps you walk each day.

    And, yes, I'm glad,
    Through smiles as well as tears
    I'm glad
    Because I want you strong
      Oh, Love, I want you strong

And good,
The man of vision
And the leader
God would have you be,
So, when the hurt must come
To help you grow
I ask but this one thing,
That God will let me
    hurt
    and grow
    with you.

I Feel Your Love

In crowded rooms
With people all around,
I feel your love:
   Oh, no——I hear no words,
   No open display
     brings warm blushes to my cheeks,
   But in the way you look at me
   You say, "I care..."
   And on my arm
   Your gentle touch
   Conveys this message to my heart:
     "To me, this one is priceless,
     My gift from God to cherish
       and protect...
     This one is mine."

In crowded rooms
With people all around,
I feel your love.

Belonging

The night is cool.
I hear a birdsong in the distance
And beneath my ear
The thudding of your heart;
Your breathing stirs my hair
And your lips,
Quietly now and undemanding,
Caress my eyes
With gentle sounds of love;
My heart responds with swelling joy
That you are mine,
That you are here,
Next to me,
Belonging,
While the fading glow
Like color in the sunset
Fills our world with sweetness
With stillness
And with rest.

The Walk

Today I walked in the quiet woods alone.
The rustle of leaves under my feet made a lonely sound
And the song of the birds was lonely too
Until I came to the old tree
With its spreading arms
And you came, too, and sat beside me.
I smiled in silent greeting
And beckoned to show you the thousands
Of tiny blue daisies looking up through the grass.
We marvelled at the lush velvet of the moss
Up close to the tree
And you hushed my voice to hear
The note of a distant bird's song.
We followed the sound as excuse
To walk under the shading arms of the old trees
Where the world seemed at peace
And quiet and still in its own thoughts.
We felt at peace, too, as we walked along,
Drinking in the solitude,
Stopping to hear the murmur of a little stream
And to watch the busy working
Of a colony of ants that caught our eye.
You stooped to let one crawl onto your finger
Where we watched his frantic searching
For companionship and security,
And we talked of his likeness with humans
Who sometimes spend a whole lifetime

Searching for something or someone to fill the void
Without ever once being satisfied.
Our steps turned back to the trail again
Under the deep shade of the old trees
And I walked beside you in silence,
Thinking of you,
Feeling a strong surge of happiness
Well up inside with such sweetness it made me ache
In thankfulness to God
For you.
I looked up to see your eyes on mine,
Deep in the same thoughts,
And you reached out to my outstretching hand
To touch my fingers
In a gentle communion of our souls;
One moment of eternity, caught and held
    in the timelessness of memory,
To be relived in months and years to come.
——One moment——then we turned and walked again
Into the hurried world.

Our Life Will Live On

In a world far removed from the rest of the world
We talked of the time
And we planned for the time
When life would begin from our love.

"How sweet it will be,"
We told ourselves,
But we didn't know
——How could we know?——
How utterly sweet the sweet would be,
How painfully deep every hurt would be,
How magnified all of our feelings would be
By the life that began
From our love.

But now that we have our little son,
This blending of you
And of me
Into one,
We know:
    Our happiness rests in these little hands,
    Our dreams in this little heart;
    Whatever he does or doesn't become,
    Whatever the race that his feet will run,
    For generations yet unborn through this son
    Our life will live on
    In this love.

Love's Acceptance

In the name of love,
    Sometimes,
Perfection is proclaimed
And blinded hearts deceive themselves,
    But blindness is not love.....

I love you
    But I see you as you are,
    Your faults, your weakness,
    The growth you need to make;
    I see the scars from broken dreams,
    The hurts, frustrations, fears.....
        And I love you,
        Not because I will not see or cannot see,
        But because I see the whole:
            Your reaching up to better things,
            Your dreams,
            Your searching of your soul
            To know yourself
            And grow.
            I see your love for others
            And for God,
            Your selfless love for me;
            I see you as you are,
            Accept you as you are,
            Love you as you are
            And for all you long to be.

Your Hurting Words

Oh——please, please——I love you——
I have no shield
Against these hurting words you say——
Oh——please——
I'd lay my fingers
On your lips
To stop the words
I cannot bear to hear;
I'd hold you
Tightly in my arms
And close this distance
You would make between our hearts
    ——hold me——
The tears that fill my soul
Are frozen by your coldness
And cannot wash the stinging
From my eyes.
Oh——unsay the words——
    unmake this gulf;
    I cannot bear this deadness
    I cannot live
    Without your love
Oh——please——turn the hours back
    and make my world all right again.

'Oh Dear Mine.....Forgive Me'

The wound was deep
Because the love was deep,
And the empty silence
Said you did not care;

The distance you had made
Was much too great
For me to span alone
And so with aching arms
And bleeding heart
I turned away
To hide the burning tears.....
    I could not make a beggar of my love.

And then I felt your nearness
    I felt your touch
I even felt the sorrow in your heart:
    "Oh dear mine
        Forgive me——please forgive me."

    .....Sweet, sweet words
      That made me whole.

In Your Absence

You've gone away
And left my world a lonely, empty void.....
   I walk through rooms we shared
   And everywhere I feel your presence,
   The echo of your voice,
   I touch the book you read,
   Listen to the song you liked so well;
   I hear again the things you said
   And feel your hand on mine,
      But, oh, you've gone
      And there's a deadness in these rooms——

I'd leave this emptiness behind——
   I walk deserted paths through trees and vines,
   ——Fast, and faster still——
   Away from anything we shared,
   But though I run I can't escape
   This empty wrenching pain:
   It isn't in the rooms
   Or in these woods,
   I can't go far enough
   Or fast enough
   To leave the hurt behind:
   A loss I've never known before
   Is in my heart.....
      You've gone
      And I'm alone.

Coldness.....Loneliness

There's a dreariness outside my window today
Like the dreariness in my heart.
Last night's rain littered the ground
With limbs and needles
   ——debris——
Like my tears that left a soggy heart
Littered with broken laughter
And the debris of happier days.

    Winter has come
    And you have gone.

Coldness
And loneliness.....
    one, physical,
    the other, emotional.....
    .....but born of the same parents
      I think.....

Such Shallow Words

"I love you"
——oh, such shallow words——
They tell you nothing
    Of this hurting depth of me,
    this pain that reaches up
    and clutches at my heart
    because you're gone.

They tell you nothing
    Of the hope
    I've made into a shield
    against despair,
    against——perhaps——reality,
    against the picture
    forming in my mind
    of lonely years,
    empty years
    when you are gone
        eternally.

"I love you"
    Oh, such shallow words.....

The Lonely Places

In the lonely places of my mind
I walk with you,
Down shadowed roads,
Beside a quiet stream,
Beneath the blackened skies
Where stars have disappeared;
I walk with you
In lonely crowds
And where the swirling snowflakes fall,
Where haunting night sounds
Fill the empty air
And trees are bent
Beneath the wind and rain;
I walk with you
And feel the peace
Without, within;
I feel your gentleness
And hear the quiet cadence
Of your voice
In companionship,
Precious, dear to me,
Wording thoughts of beauty and of strength,
Thoughts that lift my soul
And fill the lonely places of my mind.

I Wish You Were Here

I wish you were here.
 The wind is cool
 And last year's dead leaves rustle on the trees;
 Here and there a bird calls
 But,
 Mostly,
 There is a stillness.

 The whole atmosphere says,
 "Spring! Spring!"
 I want so much to share this time
 With you
 But how can
  brightness
  and sounds
  and fragrances
  and new softnesses of growth
  be put into words
  that will recreate spring
  on the other side of the world?

 I wish you were here.

Outwardly

Outwardly, I appear calm
And normal.
I'm working,
      writing letters,
      cleaning house——
No one would suspect that
      inside
Every cell is aching with excitement
And with longing!

      Your're coming home!
      Your're coming home!

45

Sharing

How much it means to me,
    This time of walking in the stillness
    Before the dark,
    Trailing footsteps,
    Admiring flowers,
    Checking little trees
    To see their growth,
    Talking of improvements
    And the work we want to do,
    Smelling roses
    And exulting in new blooms,
    Ending up at last
    Here in the swing,
    Listening to the waterfall,
    Watching stars come out
    And dusky blueness sweep the heavens,
    Talking,
    Contented,
    Filled with happiness
    For all God's perfect gifts.

How much it means to me
    To share these things with you.

Time To Rest

I stand here
In the circle of your arms,
Unmoving,
Wanting through my stillness
To stop the world
And time.

    I feel your body,
    Solid,
    Warm,
    And I feel your heart,
    A steady echo of my own;
    I feel the softness of your cheek,
    Your breath against my hair;
    I needed this,

        no hurried hug
        or brushing lips
        but this time to rest here,
        securely in your arms
        as in your heart,
        quietly,
        drawing strength
        for now
        and for tomorrows
        yet to come.

In Your Eyes

He'd gone
And I waited at the window
Looking down and down the empty street,
    Empty now
    Except for ice and snow.

My body ached in fear for him
And love,
Questioning, as I stood and cried:
    Is that cord
    Between a mother and a son
    Never really cut?
    And the hurting that a mother feels,
    The tears that fall in lonely silence
        ——No——
    A father wouldn't feel that kind of bond
    And pain.

I tried to hide it, though,
    The need to hold him close,
    The fear.....
Waiting,
Watching hours slowly pass,
Waiting
Until he calls
Until he's there
And fear can end.

And, oh, with thankful heart
I run to you
To tell you that he's safe——
You look up.....
    And in your eyes
    I see my aching fear
    And my relief
    And thankfulness.
Your hand seeks mine
As though our need for touching
Can somehow reach to him,
And I know my question's answer:
    The oneness of our love
    That gave him life
    Is no less shared tonight
    In this cord, uncut and taunt,
    That reaches out to him.

Love

Love?
It should begin like a seed
Dropped on the earth to germinate
And to spread roots slowly,
Building a slender trunk and small branches,
Growing at pace with itself,
So that, like a great oak growing to maturity,
Love will have grown
From a small nothingness
To the fulness of the heart's capacity
As that capacity has grown.
And, like the oak,
Such love sways and bends with storms of adversity
But weathers them all
And lives on
For a hundred years.

But your love?
With no gentle sprouting and growth
Did it come,
But suddenly,
As a full-grown tree,
Thrusting trunk and branches
Through the earth of my heart,
Breaking and tearing its way
To heaven's light,
Forcing root space,

Unmindful of the upheaval;
And where nothing had been,
Suddenly the proud trunk
And sweeping limbs
Were there,
Warmed in the smile of God's sunlight,
Washed by the rain of His tears,
And the earth and the sky
Of my heart space
Had to grow
To make room for you.
Yes, that was long ago.

The tears and the breaks
——So painful at first——
Mended with the years.
Washing rains and sun
Healed the earth of my heart
And brought the grass
And the flowers
To grow at your feet.
The pain has gone,
The space has grown
To fit you now,
And I wonder if such love,
So uniquely born,
Will weather stormy winds
And live eternally?

What Will We Do?

What will we do?
The question hangs in the air,
Ghost-like, between us,
Demanding an answer that no one can give.

What will we do?
The last one is leaving tomorrow——
School...
    Then marriage...
    a life of her own...

And what will we do
With no little feet tripping around,
No one to guide,
No voice in the night calling out, "Mommy",
Needing assurance,
    "Go to sleep, Honey——
    Everything is all right."
No one to wait for after a date,
No heart-to-heart talks or sharing of tears?

How still it will seem
Here in the house
And how still in our hearts
When this last one has gone.

What will we do?

How Good It's Been

Like a playful river,
Running here and there
Through shadowed forests,
Over boulders,
Out across the sandy wastes,
And back again
    to mountain valleys deep
Our lives have wandered
Through these checkered years.

We've seen so many things
And struggled
    in so many ways.
We've felt a few defeats
When doors were better closed,
And we've laughed together
With each goal
God helped us to achieve.
We've seen our children born
And watched them grow
Rejoicing in the goodness of their lives;
And while they grew
We've watched the changes in ourselves
    from young and green
    to old and gray,
Changes that have brought us
To today.

Are you thinking my thoughts, Love?
How good it's been,
The fun we've had
    through "ups and downs"
    and "thick and thin"
And laughing through the tears
Together?
And won't it be exciting
To live the coming years
Together?

We Couldn't Know

You couldn't know
And I couldn't know
All those long undeveloped years ago
How right you would be for me.

We couldn't know
How much I needed
Your gentle prods,
Your vision too big
That has kept me
Always running along in its wake;
I needed your words, unclouded by doubt,
    "Of course you can do it..."
That pushed me
Out into worlds I'd never seen
Doing the things I'd never dreamed
And growing
Whether I chose to be growing or not.

I've learned to be thankful
For courage you had
To step back and leave me
When that was the best
    or to stand close beside me,
    willing to guide me,
    when tears choked my heart
    with begging for rest.

You couldn't know
And I couldn't know
All those long undeveloped years ago
How right you would be for me

but God knew.

Growing Old In Love

I come to find you sleeping quietly,
   Dear, familiar form
   that I have known so long.
It seems unreal, somehow,
   kneeling here beside your chair,
That such a snowy head is yours
And shoulders droop
From tiredness and from time;
The hand I hold
Is weak,
   with fragile skin and spots of age.....

Oh, my love,
Was it so many yesterdays ago
That youth and strength
Filled every cell
And not a hair was white?
I see within this sleeping form
The man of early years
With proud dark head
And flashing eyes,
Infectious smile,
Shoulders strong and broad
To carry all your load
And part of mine, sometimes.
And these dear hands
——I kiss the aging skin——

61

Were deft, yet gentle still
In work and play and love.
Your step
——so feeble now——
Was firm with purpose then.
Oh, my love,
How time has flown
——these years we've lived as one——
Yet in my heart
All our goals,
All our working,
All we've struggled to achieve,
——the yesterday and now——
Are tightly bound together
Just as the youth I knew
Lives on
Inside your resting form.

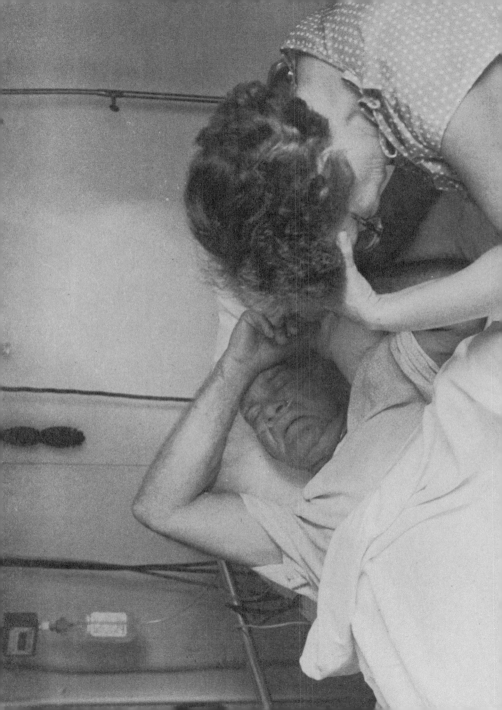

So Much Of Me

Oh, my love,
With trembling hand
I touch your cheek.
You lie so still and white,
Unhearing
All the words of love
I want to say.

Oh, dear one,
So much of me
Lies sleeping in your stillness.
I hold your hand
And wait and pray.

God hears.....
I know He hears
And feels
This bleeding of my heart,
This frantic urge
To lift you up
And hold you tightly to myself
As though
Somehow
From me to you
Could pass the health and strength
Your body needs
To make you well.....

But——oh——
There's nothing I can give of me to help
Except this hurting love
Seeking answer still
Inside your heart,
Except this will
That says that you must live
Because
     ——Oh, God——
       You made us one
       And now too much of me
       Is bound up in his life
       To live alone.

The World Without You

You live
And so, dear one,
My world has sun,
Blue skies and rainbows,
Laughter bubbling up through happy days,
A song of gladness in my heart
And peace within my soul
   Because you live.

But, oh dear one,
If you were gone
How would I mark
The weary day to follow weary day
That must be somehow passed
In living death
Before my soul could rest with yours?

How could I live
If your heart in my breast
Was still?

Goodbye

Every parting of our ways through all these years
Has had its own goodbye to ease the pain——
   The big goodbyes
      When we married and left home,
      When the kids spent summer weeks away,
      When college came, and later when they married
      And they turned with tears and waved again,
      Starting "on their own".
   The little goodbyes, too,
      Goodnights,
      A visit to a friend's,
      Going off to work each morning
      And to school...
   Separations,
   Each one with its own goodbye
   To fill the need of coming emptiness.
      That little moment of a prayer together,
      One last kiss,
      Perhaps, "I'm sorry," restoring precious peace,
      A hug, tighter for the parting.
      "I love you,"
      With a searching, telling look,
      And all the words that somehow needed to be said
      Before, "Goodbye."
  Still, the loneliness was there:
      I don't deny it——
      But not so heavy, not so hopeless

Because the words,
The lingering memory of the touch,
Were there to give us strength.

Last week
You went outside to do some work
While I made a little lunch.
I waited, thinking you would come,
And wondering
——Suddenly fearing
With a coldness and a dread——
I ran outside to find you fallen,
Lying in a stillness
That no frantic cry would move.

Oh, my love,
I am bereft

    empty

But perhaps
Perhaps
I wouldn't feel so wholly lost,
So overwhelmed with grief
If we had been allowed
That little time,
That last goodbye.

Did You Know?

Time has passed, dear one,
Since you left me in this world
To walk the way alone.
How many days or weeks?
I cannot say unless I stop and count;
I only know
That there was life when you were here
And lonely waiting
Since you've gone.

Sometimes, still,
I hear your step
Coming down the hall
Or, half asleep,
I feel your hand
Or hear your call.

And sometimes, Love,
When it can seem
You're only just away
——as so many times you were——
Then I can think to you
And live to you
And feel your living in response,
And
——with others close around——
Almost, there is normalcy.

But
.....it's like a part of me inside
        is waiting, always waiting
        with bated breath,
        and when you never come
        even though I've waited past endurance,
        that cutting blade of hurt
        is new inside again
        and wet with blood,
        or is it tears?

Oh my love,
Did you know, that day,
As you were leaving me
And all my world behind,
How hard my way would be
Alone?

Bright, Yellow Sunshine

There is sunshine today, Love,
Bright, yellow sunshine,
Warm with God's love
Pouring into my heart
And spilling over the edges
With glorious radiance,
Lighting eyes and smiles,
Shining in the caring faces
Of the ones I love,
Filling even this,
The vacuum in my soul
That was dark with grief for you.

His love is good
And sweet with healing,
Saying that the gift of love we shared
Must live
And help me find anew
The way to life.